Introduction

First of all, your support for my Christmas book, *Christmas Quilting With Wendy Sheppard* (2023), was overwhelming! Thank you, thank you!

The start of autumn always beckons hearts to return to home. I hope the autumn quilt projects in this book bring you the coziness of home and hearth, much like the comforting desserts for which the quilts are named!

I like to sort my quilts by design type. Included in this book are a few companion projects for the quilts in the Christmas book. That way, you may be able to start a collection of quilts with specific design themes as well. You will notice that a few quilts in the book do not have to be made in an autumn palette—make them one of a kind with the colors of your choice!

Happy Quilting!
Wendy

Table of Contents

Homemade Cinnamon Rolls

A cozy cabin with cats and cinnamon rolls is the perfect place to spend a chilly morning.

Skill Level
Intermediate

Finished Sizes
Quilt Size: 48" x 72"

Block Size: 8" x 8"

Number of Blocks: 48

Materials
- 2⅛ yards white print*
- ½ yard black print*
- 1 yard tan print #1*
- ⅜ yard tan print #2*
- ⅜ yard tan print #3*
- ⅜ yard tan print #4*
- ⅜ yard tan print #5*
- 1⅛ yards orange print #1*
- ⅜ yard orange print #2*
- ⅜ yard red print #1*
- ⅜ yard red print #2*
- ⅜ yard navy print #1*
- ⅜ yard navy print #2*
- 4⅞ yards backing*
- 56" x 80" batting*
- Thread*
- Basic sewing tools and supplies

*Fabric from the Daisy Lane by Kansas Troubles Quilters and Jelly & Jam by Fig Tree Quilts collections for Moda Fabrics; Tuscany Silk batting from Hobbs; Aurifil 50 wt. thread used to make sample. EQ8 was used to design this quilt.

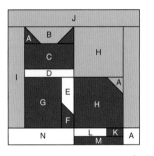

Cat
8" x 8" Finished Block
Make 3 orange
Make 5 black

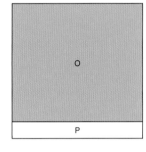

Stripe Block
8" x 8" Finished Block
Make 4

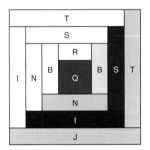

Brown Log Cabin
8" x 8" Finished Block
Make 18

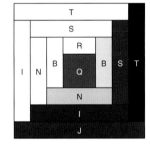

Blue Log Cabin
8" x 8" Finished Block
Make 18

Project Notes
Read all instructions before beginning this project.

Stitch right sides together using a ¼" seam allowance unless otherwise specified.

Materials and cutting lists assume 40" of usable fabric width for yardage.

Arrows indicate directions to press seams.

WOF – width of fabric

HST – half-square triangle ◻

QST – quarter-square triangle ⊠

Inspiration

"The light and dark values of the log cabin blocks and their placements in the quilt reminded me of cinnamon rolls! The reproduction fabrics used in this quilt set the stage for cozy, and the kitties lounging on the ledges definitely added to the cozy factor of this design." —Wendy Sheppard

Cutting

From white print cut:
- 3 (2" x WOF) strips, stitch short ends to short ends, then subcut into:
    2 (2" x 48½") V border strips
- 3 (1½" x WOF) strips, stitch short ends to short ends, then subcut into:
    2 (1½" x 48½") U border strips
- 4 (1½" x 8½") P rectangles
- 36 (1½" x 7½") T rectangles
- 36 (1½" x 6½") I rectangles
- 36 (1½" x 5½") S rectangles
- 44 (1½" x 4½") N rectangles
- 36 (1½" x 3½") B rectangles
- 36 (1½" x 2½") R rectangles
- 8 (1½") A squares
- 8 (1¼" x 2¾") E rectangles
- 8 (1" x 3½") D rectangles
- 8 (1" x 2½") L rectangles

From black print cut:
- 5 (3½") H squares
- 5 (2¾" x 3½") G rectangles
- 5 (2" x 3½") C rectangles
- 10 (1½") A squares
- 5 (1¼" x 2") F rectangles
- 5 (1" x 3½") M rectangles
- 5 (1" x 1½") K rectangles

From tan print #1 cut:
- 4 (7½" x 8½") O rectangles
- 8 (3½") H squares
- 3 (2" x WOF) strips, stitch short ends to short ends, then subcut into:
    2 (2" x 48½") V border strips
- 8 (1½" x 8½") J rectangles
- 16 (1½" x 6½") I rectangles
- 8 (1½" x 3½") B rectangles
- 8 (1½") A squares

From tan print #2 cut:
- 36 (1½" x 3½") B rectangles

From tan print #3 cut:
- 36 (1½" x 4½") N rectangles

From tan print #4 cut:
- 18 (1½" x 7½") T rectangles

From tan print #5 cut:
- 18 (1½" x 8½") J rectangles

From orange print #1 cut:
- 3 (3½") H squares
- 3 (2¾" x 3½") G rectangles
- 7 (2½" x WOF) binding strips
- 3 (2" x 3½") C rectangles
- 6 (1½") A squares
- 3 (1¼" x 2") F rectangles
- 3 (1" x 3½") M rectangles
- 3 (1" x 1½") K rectangles

From orange print #2 cut:
- 36 (2½") Q squares

From red print #1 cut:
- 36 (1½" x 5½") S rectangles

From red print #2 cut:
- 36 (1½" x 6½") I rectangles

From navy print #1 cut:
- 18 (1½" x 7½") T rectangles

From navy print #2 cut:
- 18 (1½" x 8½") J rectangles

Completing the Cat Blocks

1. Refer to Sew & Flip Corners on page 48 and sew two orange print #1 A squares to opposite sides of a tan print #1 B rectangle to make an A-B unit (Figure 1).

Figure 1

2. Sew an orange print #1 C rectangle to the top of a white print D rectangle; join to the bottom of the A-B unit to make an A-B-C-D unit (Figure 2).

Figure 2

3. Sew a white print E rectangle and orange print #1 F rectangle together at a 45-degree angle to make an E-F unit. Sew an orange print #1 G rectangle to the left side of the E-F unit to make an E-F-G unit (Figure 3).

E-F Unit   E-F-G Unit

Figure 3

4. Use the Sew & Flip Corners method to sew a tan print #1 A square to top right corner of an orange print #1 H square to make and A-H unit (Figure 4).

A-H Unit

Figure 4

5. Sew A-B-C-D unit to the left side of a tan print #1 H square. Sew together the E-F-G and A-H units, then sew to the bottom to complete a cat unit (Figure 5).

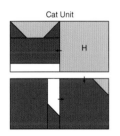

Cat Unit

Figure 5   **Figure 6**

6. Sew two tan print #1 I rectangles to opposite sides of cat unit. Sew a tan print #1 J rectangle to the top (Figure 6).

7. Sew together a white print L rectangle and an orange print #1 K rectangle. Sew an orange print #1 M rectangle to the bottom edge to make a K-L-M unit (Figure 7).

K-L-M Unit

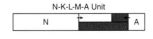

N-K-L-M-A Unit

Figure 7   **Figure 8**

8. Sew a white print N rectangle to the left side and a white print A square to the right side of K-L-M unit to make an N-K-L-M-A unit (Figure 8).

9. Sew the N-K-L-M-A unit to bottom of the step 6 unit to complete Cat block (Figure 9).

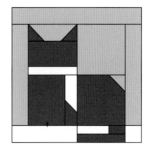

Figure 9

10. Repeat steps 1–9 to make a total of three orange Cat blocks and five black Cat blocks.

Completing the Stripe Blocks

1. Sew a white print P rectangle to the bottom of tan print #1 O rectangle to complete a Stripe block (Figure 10). Make four.

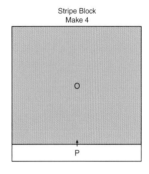

Stripe Block
Make 4

Figure 10

Completing the Log Cabin Blocks

1. Sew a white print R rectangle to the top edge of an orange print #2 Q square to make an R-Q unit. Sew a white print B rectangle to the left side and a tan print #2 B rectangle to the right side of R-Q unit to make a B-R-B-Q unit (Figure 11). Make 36.

B-R-Q-B Unit
Make 36

Figure 11

2. Sew a tan print #3 N rectangle to the bottom edge of a B-R-Q-B unit. Working in a clockwise direction, add patches in the following order, pressing after each seam: white print N rectangle, white print S rectangle, red print #1 S rectangle, red print #2 I rectangle, white print I rectangle, white print T rectangle, tan print #4 T rectangle and tan print #5 J rectangle to complete a Brown Log Cabin Block (Figure 12). Make 18.

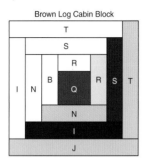

Brown Log Cabin Block

Figure 12

3. Sew a tan print #3 N rectangle to the bottom edge of a B-R-Q-B unit. Working in a clockwise direction, add patches in the following order, pressing after each seam: white print N rectangle, white print S rectangle, red print #1 S rectangle, red print #2 I rectangle, white print I rectangle, white print T rectangle, navy print #1 T rectangle and navy print #2 J rectangle to complete a Blue Log Cabin Block (Figure 13). Make 18.

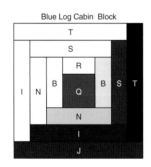

Blue Log Cabin Block

Figure 13

Completing the Quilt

1. Arrange and sew together four Cat blocks and two Stripe blocks to make a row (Figure 14). Make two.

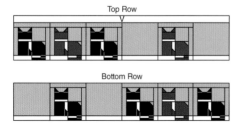

Top Row

Bottom Row

Figure 14

2. Arrange and sew together six Log Cabin blocks to make a row, watching color and orientation of blocks carefully. Make six rows. Sew rows together to complete quilt center; press (Figure 15).

Figure 15

3. Referring to the Assembly Diagram, sew two white print U strips, two cat rows, two tan print #1 V strips, two white print V strips and quilt center together.

4. Layer, baste, quilt as desired and bind referring to Quilting Basics. The photographed quilt was quilted with a floral design. ●

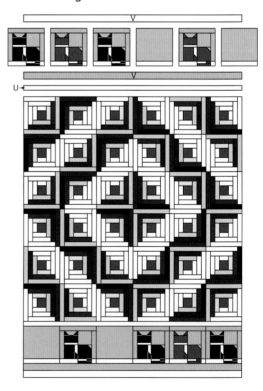

Homemade Cinnamon Rolls
Assembly Diagram 48" x 72"

Apple Petit Fours

This quilt is perfect for using up fabrics of different colors in your stash for a scrappy, sparkly look.

Quilted by Darlene Szabo of Sew Graceful Quilting

Skill Level
Intermediate

Finished Sizes
Quilt Size: 69" x 69"

Block Size: 12" x 12"

Number of Blocks: 25

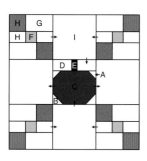

Apple
12" x 12" Finished Block
Make 12

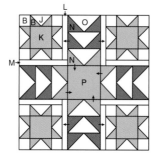

Star
12" x 12" Finished Block
Make 13

Materials
- 4¾ yards white*
- ⅔ yard yellow*
- ¾ yard green #1*
- ⅝ yard brown #1*
- ⅜ yard each orange, red #1, red #2 and aqua #1*
- ⅓ yard red #3*
- ¼ yard each brown #2 and aqua #2*
- ⅞ yard green #2*
- 4⅓ yards backing*
- 77" x 77" batting*
- Thread*
- Basic sewing tools and supplies

Fabric from the Rainbow Spice collection by Sariditty for Moda Fabrics; Aurifil 50 wt. thread; Tuscany Silk batting from Hobbs used to make sample. EQ8 was used to design this quilt.

Project Notes
Read all instructions before beginning this project.

Stitch right sides together using a ¼" seam allowance unless otherwise specified.

Materials and cutting lists assume 40" of usable fabric width for yardage.

Arrows indicate directions to press seams.

WOF – width of fabric
HST – half-square triangle ◨
QST – quarter-square triangle ⊠

Cutting

From white cut:
- 48 (4½") I squares
- 4 (2½" x WOF) G strips
- 4 (2" x WOF) H strips
- 156 (2" x 3½") O rectangles
- 40 (1½" x 12½") Q strips
- 52 (1½" x 5½") M strips
- 52 (1½" x 4½") L strips
- 208 (1½" x 2½") J rectangles
- 24 (1½" x 2¼") D rectangles
- 232 (1½") B squares
- 24 (1¼") A squares
- 7 (3" x WOF) R/S strips, stitch short ends to short ends, then subcut into:
    2 (3" x 64½") R and
    2 (3" x 69½") S strips

From yellow cut:
- 3 (3½") P squares
- 12 (2½") K squares
- 24 (2") N squares
- 2 (1½" x WOF) F strips
- 96 (1½") B squares

From green #1 cut:
- 3 (3½") P squares
- 12 (2½") K squares
- 24 (2") N squares
- 2 (2" x WOF) H strips
- 96 (1½") B squares

From brown #1 cut:
- 3 (3½") P squares
- 12 (2½") K squares
- 24 (2") N squares
- 96 (1½") B squares
- 12 (1" x 1½") E rectangles

From orange cut:
- 48 (2") N squares
- 2 (2" x WOF) H strips

From red #1 cut:
- 12 (3½" x 4½") C rectangles

From red #2 cut:
- 2 (3½") P squares
- 8 (2½") K squares
- 16 (2") N squares
- 64 (1½") B squares

From aqua #1 cut:
- 2 (2¼" x WOF) B strips
- 98 (2¼" x 7½") D rectangles
- 3 (1" x WOF) E strips

From red #3 cut:
- 32 (2") N squares
- 16 (1½" x 2½") B squares

From brown #2 cut:
- 48 (2") N squares

From aqua #2 cut:
- 32 (2") N squares

From green #2 cut:
- 48 (2") N squares
- 8 (2½" x WOF) binding strips

Completing the Blocks

Apple Blocks

1. Referring to Sew & Flip Corners on page 48, sew A squares to the top corners of the C rectangles and B squares to the bottom corners (Figure 1). Make 12.

Make 12

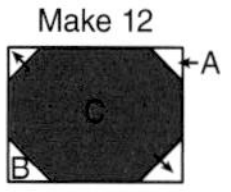

Figure 1

2. Sew two D rectangles to opposite sides of one E rectangle (Figure 2a). Make 12.

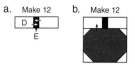
a. Make 12   b. Make 12

Figure 2

3. Sew one step 2 unit to each step 1 unit as shown (Figure 2b).

4. Sew together green #1 H and G strips along one long edge as shown to make two strip set #1's (Figure 3a). Subcut 48 (2"-wide) segment #1 units.

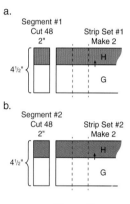
a.
Segment #1
Cut 48
2"
Strip Set #1
Make 2
4½"
H
G

b.
Segment #2
Cut 48
2"
Strip Set #2
Make 2
4½"
H
G

Figure 3

5. Repeat using orange H and G strips to cut 48 segment #2 units (Figure 3b).

6. Sew white H strips to opposite long sides of yellow F strips as shown to make two strip set #3's (Figure 4). Subcut 48 (1½"-wide) segment #3 units.

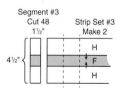
Segment #3
Cut 48
1½"
Strip Set #3
Make 2
4½"
H
F
H

Figure 4

7. Sew together one each segment #1, #2 and #3 units as shown to make one corner unit (Figure 5). Make 48.

Corner Unit
Make 48

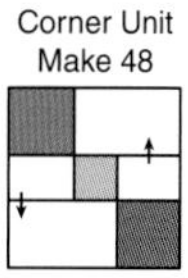

Figure 5

8. Referring to the Apple block diagram, arrange four corner units, four I squares and one step 3 unit into three rows as shown. Sew units and squares together in rows; join the rows to make one Apple block. Make 12.

Star Blocks

9. Referring to Sew & Flip Flying Geese on page 47, use yellow B squares and J rectangles to make 16 flying geese units (Figure 6).

Flying Geese Unit
Make 16

Figure 6

10. Arrange four flying geese units, four white B squares and one yellow K square in three rows as shown (Figure 7). Sew units and squares together in rows; join the rows to make one small star unit. Make four.

Small Star Unit
Make 4

Figure 7

11. Sew an L strip to the right side of one small star unit, then sew an M strip to the bottom of the unit to make one corner star unit (Figure 8). Make four.

Corner Star Unit
Make 4   L

Figure 8

12. Referring again to Sew & Flip Flying Geese, make four large flying geese units using O rectangles and yellow N squares (Figure 9a).

Large Flying   Large Flying
Geese Unit   Geese Contrast Unit
a.   Make 4   b.   Make 8

Figure 9

13. In the same manner, make eight large flying geese contrast units using O rectangles and orange N squares (Figure 9b).

Designer's Note

This quilt is perfect to hone piecing skills for making basic units, or experiment with special quilting rulers meant for making the units.

14. Sew together one large flying geese unit and two large flying geese contrast units as shown to make one stacked flying geese unit (Figure 10). Make four.

Stacked Flying Geese Unit Make 4

Figure 10

15. Referring to the Star block diagram, arrange four corner star units, four stacked flying geese units and one yellow P square in three rows as shown. Sew units and square together in rows; join the rows to make one yellow/orange Star block.

16. Repeat steps 9–15 to make 13 Star blocks in the following fabric combinations:

- Make 3 each:
  Yellow/Orange Star Blocks
  Green #1/Green #2 Star Blocks
  Brown #1/Brown #2 Star Blocks

- Make 2 each:
  Red #2/Red #3 Star Blocks
  Aqua #1/Aqua #2 Star Blocks

Completing the Quilt

1. Referring to the Assembly Diagram, arrange blocks, Q strips and red #3 B squares in rows as shown.

2. Sew the blocks, strips and squares together in rows; join the rows to complete the quilt center.

3. Sew the R and S border strips to the quilt center in alphabetical order to complete the quilt top.

4. Layer, baste, quilt as desired and bind the quilt referring to Quilting Basics. The photographed quilt was quilted with large edge-to-edge feathers. ●

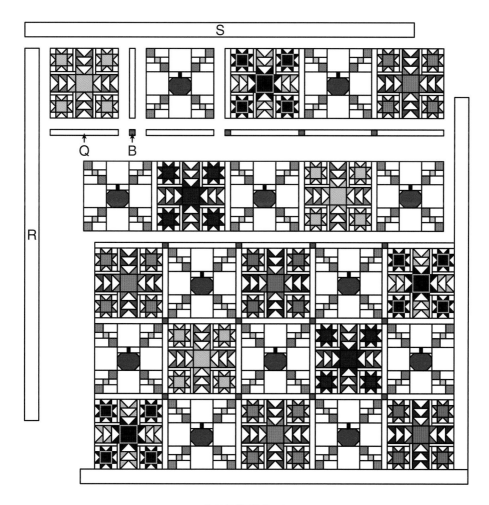

Apple Petit Fours
Assembly Diagram 69" x 69"

Blueberry Orange Bread

This stash-busting quilt uses up scraps saved from previous quilts.

Quilted by Darlene Szabo of Sew Graceful Quilting

Skill Level
Confident Beginner

Finished Sizes
Quilt Size: 60" x 60"

Block Size: 13½" x 13½"

Number of Blocks: 9

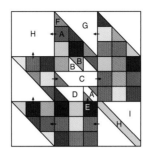

Leaf
13½" x 13½" Finished Block
Make 9

Materials
- 2⅞ yards white*
- 2⅓ yards total assorted orange, blue, navy and green print scraps or fat eighths*
- ⅝ yard apple green*
- 3⅞ yards backing*
- 68" x 68" batting*
- Thread*
- Basic sewing tools and supplies

Fabric from the Denim & Daisies and Jelly & Jam collections by Fig Tree Quilts for Moda Fabrics; Aurifil 50 wt. thread; Tuscany Silk batting from Hobbs used to make sample. EQ8 was used to design this quilt.

Project Notes
Read all instructions before beginning this project.

Stitch right sides together using a ¼" seam allowance unless otherwise specified.

Materials and cutting lists assume 40" of usable fabric width for yardage and 20" for fat eighths.

Arrows indicate directions to press seams.

WOF – width of fabric

HST – half-square triangle

QST – quarter-square triangle ⊠

Cutting

From white cut:
- 18 (5⅜") G squares, then cut once diagonally ◹
- 6 (5" x 14") J rectangles
- 3 (5" x WOF) strips, stitch short ends to short ends, then subcut into:
    2 (5" x 50") K strips
- 9 (5") H squares
- 18 (4½") I squares
- 9 (2½") B squares
- 9 (2" x 5") C rectangles
- 9 (2" x 3½") D rectangles
- 9 (2") A squares
- 6 (2¾" x WOF) L/M strips, stitch short ends to short ends then subcut into:
    2 (2¾" x 50") L and
    2 (2¾" x 54½") M strips

From assorted prints cut:
- 9 (5") H squares
- 76 (3½") N squares
- 9 (2½") B squares
- 54 (2⅜") F squares, then cut once diagonally ◹
- 297 (2") A squares
- 18 (1½") E squares

From apple green cut:
- 7 (2½" x WOF) binding strips

Completing the Blocks
1. Arrange nine assorted print A squares in three rows of three (Figure 1). Sew squares together in rows; join the rows to make one nine-patch unit. Make 18.

Nine-Patch Unit
Make 18

Figure 1

Inspiration

"After seeing a blueberry orange loaf, I was inspired to add a hint of navy into the quintessential autumn color palette for added visual interest." —Wendy Sheppard

2. Arrange three each assorted print A squares and F triangles in three rows as shown (Figure 2). Sew together in rows; join the rows to make one pieced triangle unit. Make 36.

Pieced Triangle Unit
Make 36

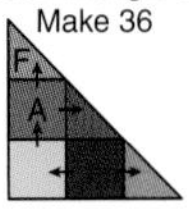

Figure 2

3. Sew one together one pieced triangle unit and one G triangle to make one pieced HST unit (Figure 3). Make 36.

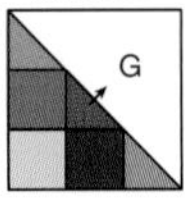

Pieced HST Unit
Make 36

Figure 3

4. Refer to Half-Square Triangles on page 46 and make 18 HST units from white and assorted print B squares (Figure 4). Trim HST units to 2" x 2", keeping the diagonal seam centered.

HST Unit
Make 18

Figure 4

5. Sew together one assorted print A square and two HST units as shown (Figure 5). Make nine.

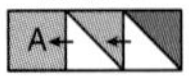

Make 9

Figure 5

6. Refer to Sew & Flip Corners on page 48 and sew one assorted print A square to a C rectangle as shown (Figure 6). Make nine.

Make 9

Figure 6

7. In the same manner, sew one assorted print A square to a D rectangle as shown (Figure 7). Make nine.

Make 9

Figure 7

8. In the same manner, sew two assorted print E squares to opposite corners of one white A square (Figure 8). Make nine.

Make 9   Make 9

Figure 8 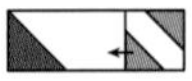   **Figure 9**

9. Sew together units from steps 7 and 8 as shown (Figure 9). Make nine.

10. Sew together one unit each from steps 5, 6 and 9 as shown to make one small leaf unit (Figure 10). Make nine.

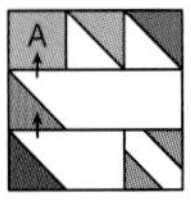

Small Leaf Unit
Make 9

Figure 10

11. Referring again to Sew & Flip Corners, sew two I squares to opposite corners of one assorted print H square to make one large stem unit (Figure 11). Make nine.

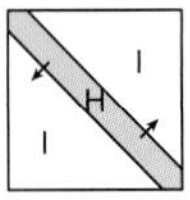

Large Stem Unit
Make 9

Figure 11

12. Referring to the Leaf block diagram, arrange four pieced HST units, two nine-patch units and one each small leaf unit, large stem unit and white H square in three rows. Join the units and square together in rows; join the rows to complete one Leaf block. Make nine.

Completing the Quilt

1. Referring to the Assembly Diagram, arrange blocks and J rectangles into three rows, noting block orientation. Sew blocks and rectangles together to make three block rows.

2. Sew block rows alternately with K strips as shown to make quilt center.

3. Sew 18 N squares together to make one side pieced outer border. Make two.

4. Sew 20 N squares together to make one top/bottom pieced outer border. Make two.

5. Sew the L and M border strips to quilt center in alphabetical order followed by the pieced outer borders to complete the quilt top.

6. Layer, baste, quilt as desired and bind referring to Quilting Basics. The photographed quilt was quilted with swirls. ●

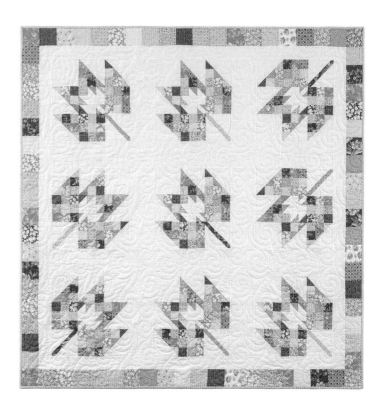

Designer's Note

Simple blocks are easily fancified when many fabrics are used. Throw in as many fabrics as you can in this quilt, and you will see your quilt sparkle!

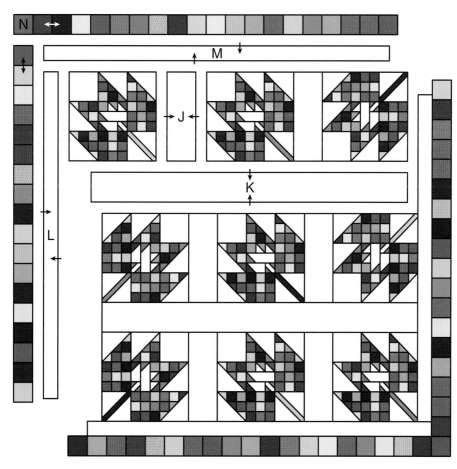

Blueberry Orange Bread
Assembly Diagram 60" x 60"

Apple Turnover

Though the quilt is sewn in a red colorway, simply use yellow, orange and brown to change the apple theme to a pumpkin theme.

Quilted by Darlene Szabo of Sew Graceful Quilting

Skill Level
Confident Beginner

Finished Sizes
Quilt Size: 69" x 69"

Block Size: 6" x 6" and 10" x 10"

Number of Blocks: 36 and 20

Materials
- 3⅞ yards white solid*
- ½ yard each red print #1, red print #2, red print #3, red print #4, tan print #1, tan print #2, tan print #3 and brown print*
- ⅞ yard red print #5*
- 1¼ yards tan print #4*
- ¼ yard dark brown print*
- 4⅞ yards backing*
- 77" x 77" batting*
- Thread*
- Basic sewing tools and supplies

*Fabric from the Lydia's Lace collection by Betsy Chutchian for Moda Fabrics; Tuscany Silk batting from Hobbs; Aurifil 50 wt. thread used to make sample. EQ8 was used to design this quilt.

Project Notes
Read all instructions before beginning this project.

Stitch right sides together using a ¼" seam allowance unless otherwise specified.

Materials and cutting lists assume 41" of usable fabric width for yardage.

Arrows indicate directions to press seams.

WOF – width of fabric
HST – half-square triangle ◱
QST – quarter-square triangle ⊠

Cutting

From white solid cut:
- 8 (3") O squares
- 7 (2½" x WOF) strips, stitch short ends to short ends, then subcut into:
    2 (2½" x 60½") Z and 2 (2½" x 64½") AA border strips
- 8 (2½" x 10½") U rectangles
- 8 (2½" x 6½") T rectangles
- 16 (2½" x 4") H rectangles
- 24 (2½") P squares
- 16 (2¼") S squares
- 32 (2") D squares
- 2 (1¾" x 36½") V border strips

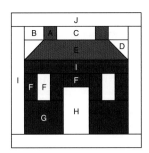

House
10" x 10" Finished Block
Make 16

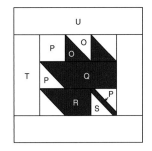

Framed Leaf
10" x 10" Finished Block
Make 4

Apple
6" x 6" Finished Block
Make 32

Leaf
6" x 6" Finished Block
Make 4

- 2 (1¾" x 39") W border strips
- 32 (1½" x 10½") J rectangles
- 32 (1½" x 8½") I rectangles
- 16 (1½" x 3½") C rectangles
- 96 (1½" x 2½") F rectangles
- 32 (1½" x 2") B rectangles
- 128 (1¼") K squares
- 64 (1" x 6½") N rectangles
- 64 (1" x 5½") M rectangles

From each red print #1, red print #3, tan print #1 and tan print #3 cut:

- 4 (4½" x 5½") L rectangles
- 1 (3") O square
- 1 (2½" x 6½") Q rectangle
- 1 (2½" x 4½") R rectangle
- 1 (2½") P square
- 4 (2" x 8½") E rectangles
- 8 (1½") A squares

From each red print #2, red print #4 and tan print #2 cut:

- 4 (4½" x 5½") L rectangles
- 8 (3" x 3½") G rectangles
- 4 (1½" x 8½") I rectangles
- 20 (1½" x 2½") F rectangles

From tan print #4 cut:

- 4 (4½" x 5½") L rectangles
- 8 (3" x 3½") G rectangles
- 7 (2½" x WOF) binding strips
- 4 (1½" x 8½") I rectangles
- 20 (1½" x 2½") F rectangles
- 2 (1¼" x 40½") Y border strips
- 2 (1¼" x 39") X border strips

From brown print cut:

- 4 (3") O squares
- 4 (2½" x 6½") Q rectangles
- 4 (2½" x 4½") R rectangles
- 4 (2½") P squares

From dark brown print cut:

- 32 (1½") A squares

From red print #5 cut:

- 7 (3" x WOF) strips, stitch short ends to short ends, then subcut into:
    2 (3" x 64½") BB and 2 (3" x 69½") CC border strips

Completing the House Blocks

1. Sew two matching print A squares to opposite sides of a white C rectangle, then sew two white B rectangles to opposite ends to make an A-B-C unit (Figure 1).

Figure 1

2. Referring to Sew & Flip Corners on page 48, sew two white D squares to the top corners of a matching print E rectangle to make a D-E unit (Figure 2a). Sew A-B-C unit to D-E unit to complete roof unit (Figure 2b).

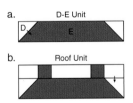

Figure 2

3. Sew together two matching print F rectangles, one white F rectangle and one matching print G rectangle to make an F-G unit (Figure 3). Make two.

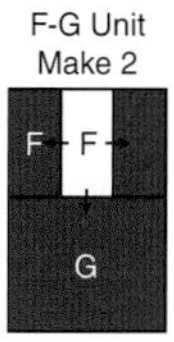

F-G Unit
Make 2

Figure 3

4. Sew one matching print F rectangle to one white H rectangle to make an F-H unit. Join two F-G units to the F-H unit to make a house unit (Figure 4).

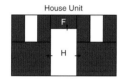

House Unit

Figure 4

5. Sew together the roof unit, one matching print I rectangle and the house unit (Figure 5).

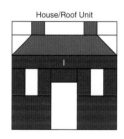

House/Roof Unit

Figure 5

6. Sew white I rectangles to the sides of the house/roof unit. Sew white J rectangles to the top and bottom of the house/roof unit to complete a House block (Figure 6).

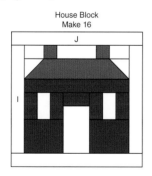

House Block
Make 16

Figure 6

7. Repeat steps 1–6 to make 16 House blocks.

Completing the Apple Blocks

1. Sew white F rectangles to opposite sides of dark brown A square to make an F-A unit (Figure 7).

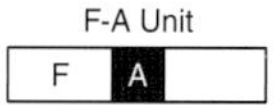

F-A Unit

Figure 7

2. Referring to Sew & Flip Corners, sew four white K squares to the corners of a print L rectangle to make a K-L unit (Figure 8).

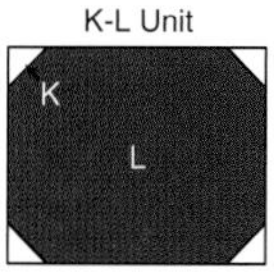

K-L Unit

Figure 8

3. Sew the F-A unit to the K-L unit. Sew white M rectangles to the sides and white N rectangles to the top and bottom to complete an Apple block (Figure 9).

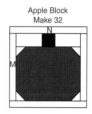

Apple Block
Make 32

Figure 9

4. Repeat steps 1–3 to make 32 Apple blocks.

Completing the Leaf Blocks

1. Refer to Half-Square Triangles on page 46 and use a white O square and a print O square to make two HST units. Trim units to 2½" x 2½". Join HST units with one white P square to make a row (Figure 10).

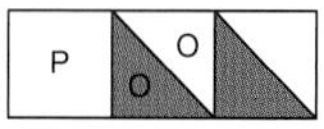

Figure 10

2. Referring to Sew & Flip Corners, sew a white P square to a matching print Q rectangle to make a P-Q unit (Figure 11).

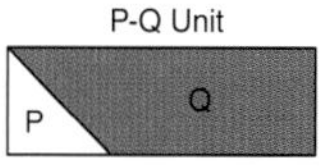

P-Q Unit

Figure 11

3. Referring to Sew & Flip Corners, sew one white P square to a matching print R rectangle. Sew two white S squares to opposite corners of a matching print P square. Join P-R unit to S-P unit to make a row (Figure 12).

Figure 12

4. Join step 1 and 3 rows and P-Q unit to complete a Leaf block (Figure 13).

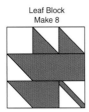

Leaf Block
Make 8

Figure 13

5. Repeat steps 1–4 to make eight Leaf blocks.

6. Sew two white T rectangles to opposite sides and two white U rectangles to top and bottom of a Leaf block to make a Framed Leaf block (Figure 14). Make four.

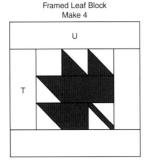

Framed Leaf Block
Make 4

Figure 14

Inspiration

"Apple turnovers are staples in my house during the autumn season. That's why I used both the apple and house blocks in this design."
—Wendy Sheppard

Completing the Quilt

1. Referring to the Assembly Diagram, lay out the Apple blocks and Leaf blocks in six rows of six blocks each, noting the placement and orientation of the blocks.

2. Sew the blocks into rows and join the rows to complete the quilt center. Press.

3. Sew the V–Y border strips to the quilt top in alphabetical order.

4. Sew together four House blocks in a vertical row. Make two and sew to the sides of the quilt center. Sew together four House blocks and two Framed Leaf blocks to make a horizontal row. Make two rows and sew to the top and bottom of the quilt center.

5. Sew the Z–CC border strips to the quilt top in alphabetical order.

6. Layer, baste, quilt as desired and bind referring to Quilting Basics. The photographed quilt was quilted with a curlicue design. ●

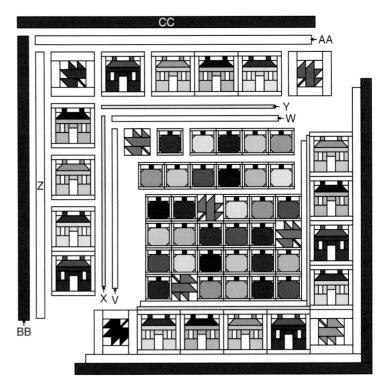

Apple Turnover
Assembly Diagram 69" x 69"

Chocolate Cream Pie

This design is perfect for a block exchange with friends.

Quilted by Darlene Szabo of Sew Graceful Quilting

Skill Level
Confident Beginner

Finished Sizes
Quilt Size: 58" x 58"

Block Size: 9" x 9"

Number of Blocks: 36

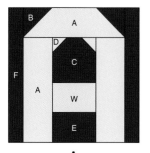

A
9" x 9" Finished Block
Make 1

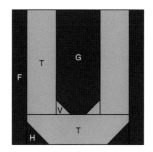

U
9" x 9" Finished Block
Make 2

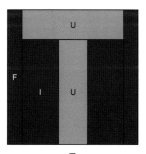

T
9" x 9" Finished Block
Make 1

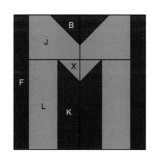

M
9" x 9" Finished Block
Make 1

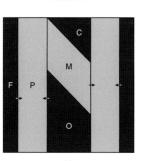

N
9" x 9" Finished Block
Make 1

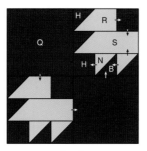

Leaf
9" x 9" Finished Block
Make 30

Materials
- 3 yards brown solid*
- 1 fat eighth or ⅛ yard each six orange prints*
- 1 fat eighth or 1 precut (10") square each 15 assorted green prints*
- 1 fat eighth or 1 precut (10") square each 15 total assorted red, orange and brown prints*
- ½ yard binding fabric*
- 3¾ yards backing*
- 66" x 66" batting*
- Thread*
- Basic sewing tools and supplies

Fabric from Jelly & Jam and Denim & Daisies collections by Fig Tree Quilts for Moda Fabrics and Bella Solids by Moda Fabrics; Aurifil 50 wt. thread; Tuscany Silk batting from Hobbs used to make sample. EQ8 was used to design this quilt.

Here's a Tip

Shop your stash for fabrics to make this quilt in a fun and scrappy look. All fabrics "pop" against a dark background!

Project Notes
Read all instructions before beginning this project.

Stitch right sides together using a ¼" seam allowance unless otherwise specified.

Materials and cutting lists assume 40" of usable fabric width for yardage and 20" for fat eighths.

Arrows indicate directions to press seams.

WOF – width of fabric
HST – half-square triangle ◻
QST – quarter-square triangle ⊠

Cutting

From length of brown solid cut:
- 2 (2½" x 58½") Z border strips
- 2 (2½" x 54½") Y border strips
- 60 (5") Q squares
- 2 (3½" x 7½") G rectangles
- 2 (3½") C squares
- 2 (3" x 7½") I rectangles
- 1 (3½" x 6") O rectangle
- 1 (2½" x 3½") E rectangle
- 64 (2½") B squares
- 2 (2" x 6½") K rectangles
- 244 (2") H squares
- 12 (1½" x 9½") F rectangles

From orange #1 cut:
- 3 (2½" x 7½") A rectangles
- 1 (2½" x 3½") W rectangle
- 2 (1½") D squares

From each orange #2 and orange #3 cut:
- 3 (2½" x 7½") T rectangles (6 total)
- 2 (1½") V squares (4 total)

From orange #4 cut:
- 2 (2½" x 7½") U rectangles

From orange #5 cut:
- 2 (3½" x 4") J rectangles
- 2 (2½" x 6½") L rectangles
- 2 (2") X squares

From orange #6 cut:
- 1 (3½" x 7") M rectangle
- 2 (2½" x 9½") P rectangles

From each assorted green, red, orange and brown prints cut:
- 2 (2½") N squares (60 total)
- 2 (2" x 5") S rectangles (60 total)
- 2 (2" x 3½") R rectangles (60 total)

From binding cut:
- 6 (2½" x WOF) binding strips

Completing the Blocks

A Block

1. Refer to Sew & Flip Corners on page 48 to add corner triangles on the upper left and upper right corners of one A rectangle using two B squares to complete the A-B unit (Figure 1a). Repeat using one C square and the D squares to complete the C-D unit (Figure 1b).

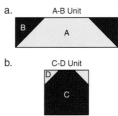

Figure 1

2. Sew the C-D unit to the top of the W rectangle and the E rectangle to the bottom, then sew the remaining A rectangles to each side. Sew the A-B unit to the top and an F rectangle to each side to complete the A block (Figure 2).

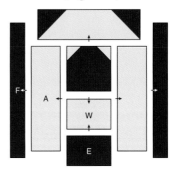

Figure 2

U Blocks

1. Refer again to Sew & Flip Corners to add corner triangles on the lower left and lower right corners of one G rectangle using two matching V squares to complete one G-V unit (Figure 3a). Repeat using one T rectangle and two H squares to complete one T-H unit (Figure 3b). Make two of each.

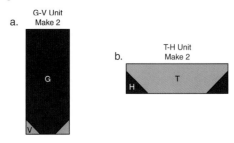

Figure 3

2. Using matching units, sew a T rectangle to each long side of one G-V unit, then sew a T-H unit to the bottom. Sew an F rectangle to each side to complete one U block (Figure 4). Make two.

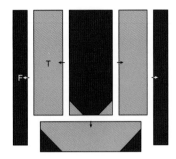

Figure 4

T Block

1. Sew the I rectangles to each long side of one U rectangle, then sew the remaining U rectangle to the top. Sew an F rectangle to each side to complete the T block (Figure 5).

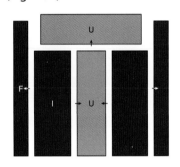

Figure 5

M Block

1. Refer again to Sew & Flip Corners to add a corner triangle on the upper right corner of one J rectangle using a B square to complete the Left J-B unit (Figure 6a). Repeat, positioning B on the upper left corner of J to make the Right J-B unit (Figure 6b). Noting fabric orientation, sew the Left J-B unit to the left of the Right J-B unit to complete the J-B section (Figure 6c).

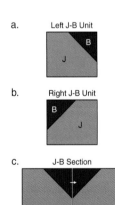

Figure 6

2. Repeat step 1 using the K rectangles and X squares to complete the K-X section (Figure 7).

Figure 7

3. Sew the L rectangles to each long side of the K-X section, then sew the J-B section to the top. Sew an F rectangle to each side to complete the M block (Figure 8).

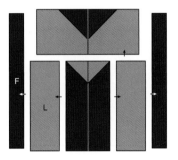

Figure 8

N Block

1. Refer again to Sew & Flip Corners to add a corner triangle on the upper right corner of the M rectangle using the remaining C square (Figure 9a).

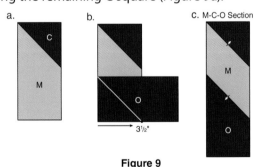

Figure 9

2. Position the O rectangle perpendicular on the lower left corner of the step 1 unit. Measure and mark a dot 3½" to the right of the lower left corner of O, then draw a diagonal line from the upper left corner of O to the dot (Figure 9b). Sew on the drawn line, then trim the seam to ¼" to complete the M-C-O section (Figure 9c).

3. Sew the P rectangles to each side of the M-C-O section, then sew the remaining F rectangles to each side to complete the N block (Figure 10).

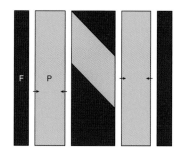

Figure 10

Leaf Blocks

1. Refer to Half-Square Triangles on page 46 to make two B-N units using one each B and N square (Figure 11). Trim the units to 2" x 2". Make 120.

B-N Unit
Make 120

Figure 11

2. Refer again to Sew & Flip Corners to add a corner triangle on the upper left corner of one R rectangle using an H square to complete one R-H unit (Figure 12a). Make 60.

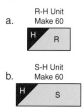

a.
R-H Unit
Make 60

b.
S-H Unit
Make 60

Figure 12

3. Repeat step 2 to make 60 S-H units using 60 each S rectangles and H squares (Figure 12b).

4. Using matching units and noting fabric orientation, arrange one R-H unit, one S-H unit, two B-N units and two H squares in three rows; sew into rows then sew the rows together to complete one leaf section (Figure 13). Make 60.

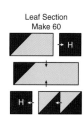

Leaf Section
Make 60

Figure 13

5. Noting fabric orientation, arrange two matching leaf sections and two Q squares in two rows; sew into rows then sew the rows together to complete one Leaf block (Figure 14). Make 30.

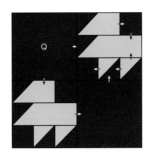

Figure 14

Here's a Tip

Spin four-patch seams to remove seam allowance bulk and create flatter blocks. Refer to Spinning Centers to Reduce Bulk on page 46 to make the seams rotate around the center point.

Completing the Quilt

1. Referring to the Assembly Diagram, arrange the letter blocks and Leaf blocks in six rows; sew into rows, then sew the rows together to complete the quilt center.

2. Sew the Y border strips to the sides of the quilt center and the Z border strips to the top and bottom to complete the quilt top.

3. Layer, baste, quilt as desired and bind referring to Quilting Basics. The photographed quilt was quilted with a diagonal edge-to-edge rounded square design. ●

Chocolate Cream Pie
Assembly Diagram 58" x 58"

Pumpkin Pancakes

This is a versatile design that can be used throughout the seasons.

Quilted by Darlene Szabo of Sew Graceful Quilting

Skill Level
Confident Beginner

Finished Sizes
Quilt Size: 60" x 75"

Block Size: 7½" x 7½"

Number of Blocks: 63

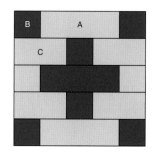

Cross
7½" x 7½" Finished Block
Make 32

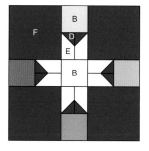

Inner Star
7½" x 7½" Finished Block
Make 17

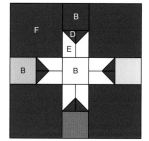

Outer Star
7½" x 7½" Finished Block
Make 14

Materials
- 3¼ yards blue print*
- 8 total assorted brown and orange fat quarters*
- ⅞ yard cream print*
- ¾ yard blue and white print*
- 5 yards backing*
- 68" x 83" batting*
- Thread*
- Basic sewing tools and supplies

*Fabric from the Denim & Daisies collection by Fig Tree Quilts for Moda Fabrics; Aurifil 50 wt. thread; Tuscany Silk batting from Hobbs used to make sample. EQ8 was used to design this quilt.

Project Notes

Read all instructions before beginning this project.

Stitch right sides together using a ¼" seam allowance unless otherwise specified.

Materials and cutting lists assume 40" of usable fabric width for yardage and 20" for fat quarters.

Arrows indicate directions to press seams.

WOF – width of fabric
HST – half-square triangle
QST – quarter-square triangle

Cutting

From blue print cut:
- 124 (3½") F squares
- 7 (2¾" x WOF) strips, stitch short ends to short ends, then subcut into:
  2 (2¾" x 71") H and 2 (2¾" x 60½") I border strips
- 14 (2" x 8") G rectangles
- 32 (2" x 5") A rectangles
- 36 (2" x 3½") C rectangles
- 210 (2") B squares
- 248 (1¼") D squares

From each brown and orange fat quarter cut*:
- 8 (2" x 5") A rectangles
- 16 (2" x 3½") C rectangles
- 8 (2") B squares
*Set aside scraps for use later.

From cream print cut:
- 31 (2") B squares
- 248 (1¼" x 2") E rectangles

From blue and white print cut:
- 7 (2½" x WOF) binding strips

Completing the Cross Blocks

Note: *Use one set of matching brown or orange prints for steps 1–4.*

1. Sew two blue B squares to opposite ends of a brown or orange A rectangle (Figure 1). Make two.

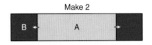

Figure 1

2. Sew two brown or orange C rectangles to opposite ends of a blue B square (Figure 2). Make two.

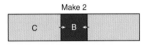

Figure 2

3. Sew two brown or orange B squares to opposite ends of a blue A rectangle (Figure 3). Make one.

Figure 3

4. Sew step 1–3 units together in rows to complete a Cross block (Figure 4).

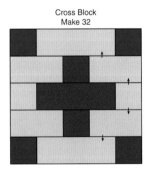

Figure 4

5. Repeat steps 1–4 to make four blocks from each group of brown and orange patches for a total of 32 Cross blocks.

6. Lay out Cross blocks on a large flat surface or design wall, leaving space for Star blocks in between as shown (Figure 5).

Figure 5

Completing the Star Blocks

Note: For best results, work on one Star block at a time in order to be able to match brown and orange B squares up with adjacent Cross blocks. Using scraps from brown and orange fat quarters, cut (2") B squares for Star blocks as you make each block.

1. Refer to Sew & Flip Corners on page 48 and sew a blue D square to top right corner of a cream E rectangle to make a unit. Make four. In the same manner, make four mirror-image units. Sew one unit to one mirror-image unit; press seam open to complete a star unit (Figure 6). Make four.

Star Unit
Make 4

Figure 6

2. Choose an empty space in the interior of the quilt layout and cut four (2") brown or orange B squares to match adjacent Cross blocks. Sew a B square to the top edge of a star unit to make a brown or orange unit (Figure 7). Make four.

Brown/Orange Unit
Make 4

Figure 7

3. Sew four blue F squares, four brown or orange units and one cream B square into three rows; join rows to complete an Inner Star block, making sure the brown or orange squares match the adjacent blocks (Figure 8).

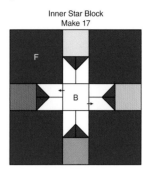

Inner Star Block
Make 17

Figure 8

4. Repeat steps 1–3 to make 17 Inner Star blocks.

5. Repeat steps 1 and 2 to make four star units and three brown or orange units. Sew together the remaining star unit and one blue B square to make one blue unit (Figure 9).

Blue Unit
Make 1

Figure 9

6. Sew four blue F squares, three brown/orange units, one blue unit and one cream B square into three rows; join rows to complete an Outer Star block (Figure 10).

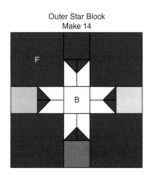

Outer Star Block
Make 14

Figure 10

7. Repeat steps 5 and 6 to make 14 Outer Star blocks.

Completing the Quilt

1. Sew the blocks into rows and join the rows to complete the quilt center; press (Figure 11).

Figure 11

2. Refer to the Assembly Diagram for the following steps. Lay quilt center on a large flat surface or design wall. Along each long edge of the quilt, lay out 10 blue C rectangles and four blue G rectangles as shown. Cut five (2") brown or orange B squares to match adjacent Cross blocks. Sew together as shown to make pieced side border. Make two and join to the quilt center.

3. Repeat using two blue B squares, eight blue C rectangles, 4 brown or orange B squares and three blue G squares to make pieced top/bottom border. Make two and join to quilt center.

4. Sew the H and I border strips to the quilt top in alphabetical order.

5. Layer, baste, quilt as desired and bind referring to Quilting Basics. The photographed quilt was quilted with an overall looping design. ●

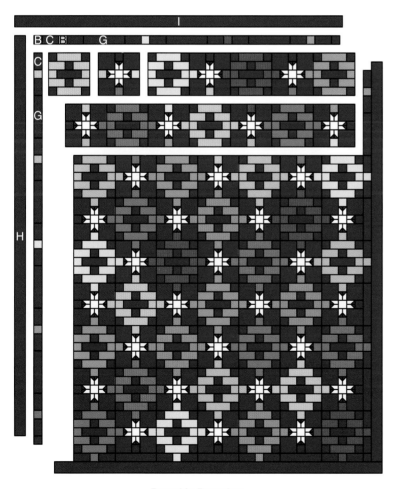

Pumpkin Pancakes
Assembly Diagram 60" x 75"

Inspiration

"I like navy for home decor. I thought: Why not mix in touches of orange for a fall sofa quilt?" —Wendy Sheppard

Italian Cream Cake

The blocks in this quilt are reminiscent of slices of Italian cream cake, with chocolate in between the layers!

Skill Level
Confident Beginner

Finished Sizes
Quilt Size: 55" x 66"

Block Size: 7" x 7", 4" x 7" and 4" x 4"

Number of Blocks: 30, 49 and 20

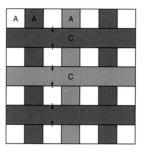

Cornerstone
4" x 4" Finished Block
Make 20

Pieced
7" x 7" Finished Block
Make 30

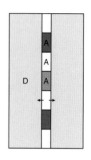

Sashing
4" x 7" Finished Block
Make 49

Materials
- 1⅞ yards cream*
- 1⅞ yards brown*
- 1¼ yards check*
- 1¾ yards beige stripe*
- 3½ yards backing*
- 63" x 74" batting*
- Thread*
- Basic sewing tools and supplies

*Fabric from the Favorite Things collection by Cheri & Chelsi for Moda Fabrics; Aurifil 50 wt. thread; Tuscany Silk batting from Hobbs used to make sample. EQ8 was used to design this quilt.

Project Notes
Read all instructions before beginning this project.

Stitch right sides together using a ¼" seam allowance unless otherwise specified.

Materials and cutting lists assume 40" of usable fabric width for yardage.

Arrows indicate directions to press seams.

WOF – width of fabric
HST – half-square triangle ◻
QST – quarter-square triangle ⊠

Cutting

From cream cut:
- 24 (1½" x WOF) A strips
- 1 (1" x WOF) E strip
- 7 (2½" x WOF) F/G strips, stitch short ends to short ends, then subcut into:
    2 (2½" x 62½") F and
    2 (2½" x 55½") G border strips

From brown cut:
- 12 (1½" x WOF) A strips
- 60 (1½" x 7½") C rectangles
- 7 (2½" x WOF) binding strips

From check cut:
- 6 (1½" x WOF) A strips
- 30 (1½" x 7½") C rectangles
- 6 (2¼" x WOF) B strips

From beige stripe cut:
- 2 (2¼" x WOF) B strips
- 98 (2¼" x 7½") D rectangles
- 3 (1" x WOF) E strips

Completing the Blocks

Pieced & Sashing Blocks

1. Sew together four cream, two brown and one check A strips along the long edges to make strip set #1 (Figure 1). Make six. Subcut 120 (1½"-wide) unit A segments and 49 (1"-wide) unit B segments from strip sets.

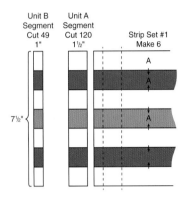

Figure 1

2. Refer to the Pieced block diagram and sew together four unit A segments, and two brown and one check C rectangles to complete one Pieced block. Make 30.

3. Refer to the Sashing block diagram and sew two beige D rectangles to opposite long sides of one unit B segment to complete one Sashing block. Make 49.

Cornerstone Blocks

1. Sew together two check B strips and one beige E strip along the long edges to make strip set #2 (Figure 2). Make three. Subcut 40 (2¼"-wide) unit C segments.

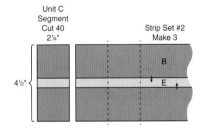

Figure 2

2. Sew together two beige B strips and one cream E strip along the long edges to make strip set #3 (Figure 3). Subcut 20 (1"-wide) unit D segments.

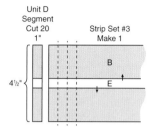

Figure 3

3. Refer to the Cornerstone block diagram and sew together two unit C segments and one unit D segments to complete one Cornerstone block. Make 20.

Completing the Quilt

1. Referring to the Assembly Diagram, sew together five Pieced blocks alternately with four Sashing blocks to make a block row. Make six.

2. In the same manner, sew together five Sashing blocks alternately with four Cornerstone blocks to make a sashing row. Make five.

3. Sew together block rows and sashing rows to complete the quilt center.

4. Sew the border strips to the quilt center in alphabetical order to complete the quilt top.

5. Layer, baste, quilt as desired and bind the quilt referring to Quilting Basics. The photographed quilt was quilted with large swirls. ●

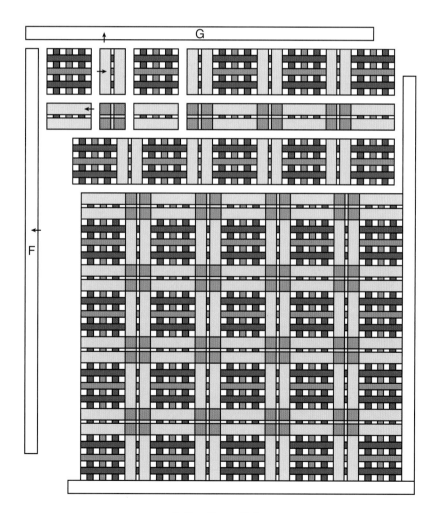

Italian Cream Cake
Assembly Diagram 55" x 66"

Pecan Pie

The colors of this quilt will make you want to enjoy a cup of coffee and a piece of homemade pecan pie with whipped topping.

Quilted by Darlene Szabo of Sew Graceful Quilting

Skill Level
Confident Beginner

Finished Sizes
Quilt Size: 58" x 75"

Block Size: 12" x 20"

Number of Blocks: 12

Materials
- 2½ yards white solid*
- ⅜ yard each light tan tonal and dark rose, taupe, medium tan and light tan prints*
- ⅝ yard light pink and cream prints*
- ¼ yard each navy, dark brown, medium brown and caramel prints*
- ¾ yard border print*
- ½ yard binding*
- 4¾ yards backing*
- 66" x 83" batting*
- Thread*
- Basic sewing tools and supplies

Fabric from the Folk & Lore collection by Fancy That Design House for Moda Fabrics; Aurifil 50 wt. thread; Tuscany Silk batting from Hobbs used to make sample. EQ8 was used to design this quilt.

Project Notes
Read all instructions before beginning this project.

Stitch right sides together using a ¼" seam allowance unless otherwise specified.

Materials and cutting lists assume 40" of usable fabric width for yardage.

Arrows indicate directions to press seams.

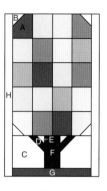

Tree
12" x 20" Finished Block
Make 8

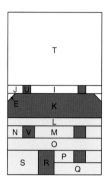

House
12" x 20" Finished Block
Make 4

WOF – width of fabric

HST – half-square triangle

QST – quarter-square triangle

Cutting

From length of white solid cut:
- 2 (3" x 65½") W border strips
- 2 (3" x 53½") X border strips
- 2 (3" x 48½") AA strips
- 4 (9½" x 12½") T rectangles
- 16 (4½") C squares
- 32 (2") B squares
- 16 (1½" x 20½") H rectangles
- 4 (1½" x 6½") I rectangles
- 8 (1½" x 2½") J rectangles
- 24 (1½") E squares

From each light tan tonal, dark rose print and taupe print cut:
- 24 (3" x 3½") A rectangles (72 total)

From each medium tan print and light tan print cut:
- 32 (3" x 3½") A rectangles (64 total)

From each light pink print and cream print cut:
- 2 (3½" x 4½") S rectangles (4 total)
- 2 (2" x 12½") O rectangles (4 total)
- 2 (2" x 6½") Q rectangles (4 total)
- 2 (2" x 5½") M rectangles (4 total)
- 2 (2" x 3") P rectangles (4 total)
- 6 (2" x 2½") N rectangles (12 total)
- 2 (1½" x 12½") L rectangles (4 total)

From remaining light pink print cut:
- 24 (3" x 3½") A rectangles

From each navy print and dark brown print cut:
- 2 (3½" x 12½") K rectangles (4 total)
- 2 (2½" x 3½") R rectangles (4 total)
- 6 (2") V squares (12 total)
- 4 (1½") U squares (8 total)

From medium brown print cut:
- 8 (2½" x 4½") F rectangles
- 16 (2½") D squares

From caramel print cut:
- 8 (1½" x 10½") G rectangles

From border print cut:
- 7 (3" x WOF) strips, stitch short ends to short ends, then subcut into:
  - 2 (3" x 70½") Y and 2 (3" x 58½") Z strips

From binding cut:
- 7 (2½" x WOF) binding strips

Completing the Blocks

Tree Blocks

1. Arrange 20 assorted A rectangles in five rows; sew into rows then sew the rows together. Refer to Sew & Flip Corners on page 48 to add corner triangles on all four corners using four B squares to complete one treetop section (Figure 1). Make eight.

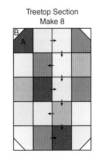

Treetop Section
Make 8

Figure 1

2. Refer again to Sew & Flip Corners to add a corner triangle on the upper right corner of one C square using a D square. Then add a corner triangle on the D square using an E square to complete one left C-D-E unit (Figure 2a). Make eight.

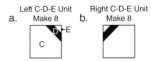

Left C-D-E Unit
Make 8

Right C-D-E Unit
Make 8

Figure 2

3. Repeat step 2 but position the corner triangles on the upper left corner of C to complete eight right C-D-E units (Figure 2b).

4. Sew a left C-D-E unit to the left long edge of one F rectangle, then sew a right C-D-E unit to the right. Sew a treetop unit to the top and a G rectangle to the bottom. Then sew H rectangles to each side to complete one Tree block (Figure 3). Make eight.

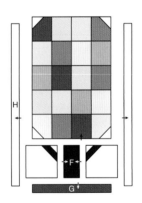

Figure 3

House Blocks

1. To make one House block, gather the following matching pieces: one each L, M, O, P, Q and S rectangles and three N rectangles. Also gather the following matching pieces: one each K and R rectangles, two U squares and three V squares.

2. Refer again to Sew & Flip Corners to add corner triangles on the upper left and upper right corner of the K rectangle using two E squares to complete the K-E unit (Figure 4).

K-E Unit

Figure 4

3. Sew the P rectangle to the left of one V rectangle and one N rectangle to the right. Then sew the Q rectangle to the bottom to complete the P-V-N-Q unit (Figure 5).

Figure 5

4. Arrange the remaining gathered pieces, the K-E unit, the P-V-N-Q unit, two J rectangles and one each T and I rectangle in seven rows; sew into rows then sew the rows together to complete one House block (Figure 6).

5. Repeat steps 1–4 to complete four House blocks.

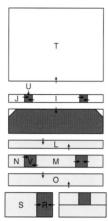

Figure 6

Completing the Quilt

1. Referring to the Assembly Diagram, arrange the Tree blocks, House blocks and two AA strips in five rows; sew into rows then sew the rows together to complete the quilt center.

2. Sew the W–Z border strips onto the quilt center in alphabetical order to complete the quilt top.

3. Layer, baste, quilt as desired and bind referring to Quilting Basics. The photographed quilt was quilted with a swirly leaf design. ●

Inspiration

"This cottage by trees design is inspired partly by the beautiful wooded neighborhoods in my area." —Wendy Sheppard

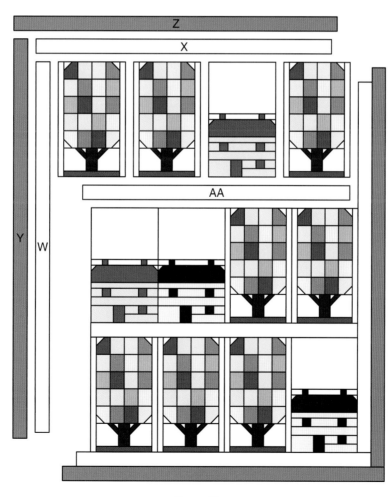

Pecan Pie
Assembly Diagram 58" x 75"

Pumpkin Pie

Although this is a two-color solids quilt, it can be made scrappy by using different print fabric scraps of two colors.

Quilted by Darlene Szabo of Sew Graceful Quilting

Skill Level
Intermediate

Finished Sizes
Quilt Size: 72" x 72"

Block Size: 12" x 12"

Number of Blocks: 25

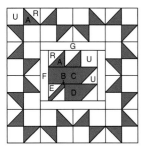

Small Leaf
12" x 12" Finished Block
Make 16

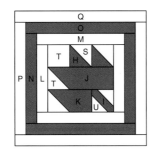

Large Leaf
12" x 12" Finished Block
Make 9

Materials
- 4¼ yards each orange and white solid*
- 4½ yards backing*
- ¾ yard dark orange solid*
- 80" x 80" batting*
- Thread*
- Basic sewing tools and supplies

Fabric from Bella Solids by Moda Fabrics; Aurifil 50 wt. thread; Tuscany Silk batting from Hobbs used to make sample. EQ8 was used to design this quilt.

Project Notes
Read all instructions before beginning this project.

Stitch right sides together using a ¼" seam allowance unless otherwise specified.

Materials and cutting lists assume 40" of usable fabric width for yardage.

Arrows indicate directions to press seams.

WOF – width of fabric

HST – half-square triangle ◺

QST – quarter-square triangle ⊠

Cutting

From length of orange solid cut:
- 4 (2½" x 80") border strips

Note: *Individual border lengths will be determined after the quilt center is completed.*

- 3 (18½") V squares, then cut twice diagonally ⊠
- 2 (9½") W squares, then cut once diagonally ◺
- 52 (5") A squares
- 9 (3") H squares
- 9 (2½" x 6½") J rectangles
- 9 (2½" x 4½") K rectangles
- 9 (2½") I squares
- 16 (2" x 5") C rectangles
- 16 (2" x 3½") D rectangles
- 16 (2") B squares
- 18 (1½" x 10½") O rectangles
- 18 (1½" x 8½") N rectangles

From white solid cut:
- 52 (5") R squares
- 9 (3") S squares
- 27 (2½") T squares
- 450 (2") U squares
- 32 (1¾") E squares
- 18 (1½" x 12½") Q rectangles
- 18 (1½" x 10½") P rectangles
- 18 (1½" x 8½") M rectangles
- 18 (1½" x 6½") L rectangles
- 32 (1¼" x 6½") G rectangles
- 32 (1¼" x 5") F rectangles

From dark orange cut:
- 8 (2½" x WOF) binding strips

Completing the Blocks

Small Leaf Block

1. Refer to Eight-at-a-Time Half-Square Triangles on page 47 to make eight A-R units using one each A and R square (Figure 1). Trim the units to 2" x 2". Make 416.

A-R Unit
Make 416

Figure 1

2. Refer to Sew & Flip Corners on page 48 to add a corner triangle on the lower right corner of one C rectangle using a U square to complete one C-U unit (Figure 2a). Repeat to make a D-U unit using one each D rectangle and U square (Figure 2b). Make 16 of each.

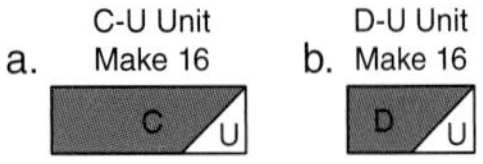

a. b.

C-U Unit
Make 16

D-U Unit
Make 16

Figure 2

3. Refer again to Sew & Flip Corners to add corner triangles on the upper left corner and lower right corner of one B square using two E squares to complete one B-E unit (Figure 3). Make 16.

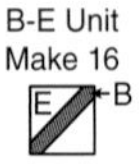

B-E Unit
Make 16

Figure 3

4. Arrange two A-R units, and one each U square, C-U unit, D-U unit and B-E unit in three rows; sew into rows then sew the rows together. Sew F rectangles to each side, then sew G rectangles to the top and bottom to complete one small leaf section (Figure 4). Make 16.

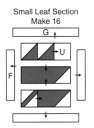

Small Leaf Section
Make 16

Figure 4

5. Arrange two each A-R units and U squares in two rows; sew into rows then sew the rows together to complete one four-patch unit (Figure 5). Make 192.

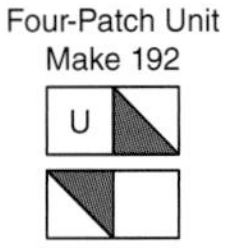

Four-Patch Unit
Make 192

Figure 5

6. Noting fabric orientation, arrange one small leaf section and 12 four-patch units in three rows. First sew the four-patch units on each side of the small leaf section together, then sew the units into rows. Sew the rows together to complete one Small Leaf block (Figure 6). Make 16.

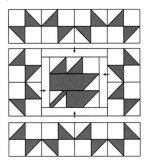

Figure 6

Large Leaf Block

1. Refer to Half-Square Triangles on page 46 to make two H-S units using one each H and S square (Figure 7). Trim the units to 2½" x 2½". Make 18.

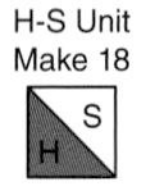

H-S Unit
Make 18

Figure 7

2. Refer again to Sew & Flip Corners to add a corner triangle on the lower left corner of one J rectangle using a T square to complete one J-T unit (Figure 8a). Repeat to make a K-T unit using one each K rectangle and T square (Figure 8b). Make nine of each.

Figure 8

3. Refer again to Sew & Flip Corners to add corner triangles on the upper right corner and lower left corner of one I square using two U squares to complete one I-U unit (Figure 9). Make nine.

Figure 9

4. Arrange two H-S units, and one each T square, J-T unit, K-T unit and I-U unit in three rows; sew into rows then sew the rows together. Sew the L–Q strips onto the unit in alphabetical order to complete one Large Leaf block (Figure 10). Make nine.

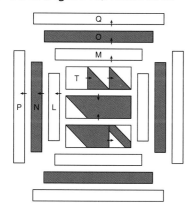

Figure 10

Completing the Quilt

1. Referring to the Assembly Diagram, arrange the Small Leaf blocks, Large Leaf blocks, V triangles and W triangles in nine diagonal rows, alternating the blocks in each row. Sew into diagonal rows, then sew the rows together. ***Note:*** *The setting triangles are cut larger and will be trimmed in the next step.*

2. Lay the patchwork on a flat surface, then trim the edges and square up the corners, leaving a ¼" seam allowance and taking care to avoid cutting through stitches, to complete the quilt center (Figure 11). After trimming and while the quilt center is laid out flat, refer to Determining Border Lengths on page 44 to measure and cut borders from the border strips.

Figure 11

3. Sew the side border strips to the side edges of the quilt center and the top and bottom border strips to the top and bottom edges to complete the quilt top.

4. Layer, baste, quilt as desired and bind referring to Quilting Basics. The photographed quilt was quilted with an echoing arc design. ●

Pumpkin Pie
Assembly Diagram 72" x 72"

DETERMINING BORDER LENGTHS

To measure for straight, plain borders:

1. Lay the pieced quilt top on a flat surface.

2. Measure the quilt top through the center from top to bottom. Side borders will be cut to this length and sewn to opposite sides of quilt top before adding top and bottom borders.

3. Measure the quilt top through the center from side to side. Add twice the finished width of the side borders plus ½" for seams to this measurement to determine the length to cut the top and bottom borders.

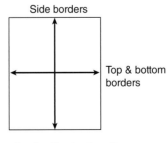

Measuring for Border Lengths

4. Borders can be cut along the lengthwise grain or crosswise grain of the fabric. A lengthwise cut will give you borders with no seams cut the total length needed. A crosswise cut requires that you cut the fabric width into strips to total the length of the border and then stitch them together to make the total length needed.

Note: If making mitered borders, add at least twice the border width to border lengths. ●

Quilting Basics

The following is a reference guide. For more information, consult a comprehensive quilting book.

Quilt Backing & Batting

Cut your backing and batting 8" larger than the finished quilt-top size and 4" larger for quilts smaller than 50" square. **Note:** *Check with longarm quilter about their requirements, if applicable. For baby quilts not going to a longarm quilter 4"–6" overall may be sufficient.* If preparing the backing from standard-width fabrics, remove the selvages and sew two or three lengths together; press seams open. If using 108"-wide fabric, trim to size on the straight grain of the fabric. Prepare batting the same size as your backing.

Quilting

1. Press quilt top on both sides and trim all loose threads. **Note:** *If you are sending your quilt to a longarm quilter, contact them for specifics about preparing your quilt for quilting.*
2. Mark quilting design on quilt top. Make a quilt sandwich by layering the backing right side down, batting and quilt top centered right side up on flat surface and smooth out. Baste layers together using pins, thread basting or spray basting to hold. **Note:** *Tape or pin backing to surface to hold taut while layering and avoid puckers.*
3. Quilt as desired by hand or machine. Remove pins or basting as you quilt.
4. Trim batting and backing edges even with raw edges of quilt top.

Binding the Quilt

1. Join binding strips on short ends with diagonal seams to make one long strip; trim seams to ¼" and press seams open (Figure 1).

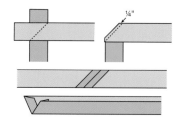

Figure 1

2. Fold ½" of one short end to wrong side and press. Fold the binding strip in half with wrong sides together along length, again referring to Figure 1; press.
3. Starting about 3" from the folded short end, sew binding to quilt top edges, matching raw edges and using a ¼" seam. Stop stitching ¼" from corner and backstitch (Figure 2).

Figure 2

4. Fold binding up at a 45-degree angle to seam and then down even with quilt edges, forming a pleat at corner (Figure 3).

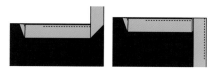

Figure 3

5. Resume stitching from corner edge as shown in Figure 3, down quilt side, backstitching ¼" from next corner. Repeat, mitering all corners, stitching to within 3" of starting point.
6. Trim binding, leaving enough length to tuck inside starting end and complete stitching (Figure 4).

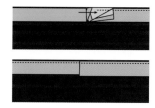

Figure 4

7. If stitching binding by hand, machine-sew binding to the front of the quilt and fold to the back before stitching. If stitching by machine, machine-sew binding to back of the quilt and fold to the front before stitching.

SPINNING CENTERS TO REDUCE BULK

When sewing a block where numerous points meet together, there can be a lot of "bulk" in the seam allowance on the wrong side of the fabric. This extra bulk prohibits the block from lying flat when pressed. One option is to trim the points off, thus reducing the amount of fabric in the seam allowance. Another option is to "spin" the center of the seam allowances, thus distributing the bulk more evenly.

1. Stitch the block as usual, nesting seams at any intersection (Photo A).

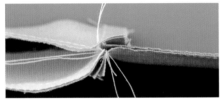

Photo A

2. Before pressing, remove approximately three stitches in the seam allowance from each side of the previously sewn seams (Photo B).

Photo B

3. Place the block on a pressing board right side down (Photo C).

Photo C

4. With your finger, push the top seam to the right and the bottom seam to the left (Photo D). This will result in the seam allowances spinning in a clockwise direction.

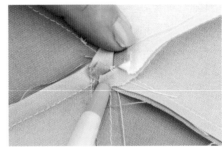

Photo D

5. The center will pop open and the seam allowances will swirl around the center of the block. Press with an iron to flatten the seam allowances in place (Photos E and F). ●

Photo E

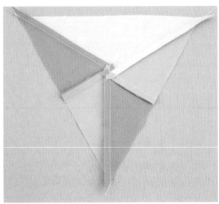

Photo F

HALF-SQUARE TRIANGLES

Half-square triangles (HSTs) are a basic unit of quilting used in many blocks or on their own. This construction method will yield two HSTs.

1. Refer to the pattern for size to cut squares. The standard formula is to add ⅞" to the finished size of the square. Cut two squares from different colors this size. For example, for a 3" finished HST unit, cut 3⅞" squares.

2. Draw a diagonal line from corner to corner on the wrong side of the lightest

color square. Layer the squares right sides together. Stitch ¼" on either side of the drawn line (Figure A).

Figure A

3. Cut the squares apart on the drawn line, leaving a ¼" seam allowance and making two HST units referring to Figure B.

Figure B

4. Open the HST units and press seam allowances toward the darker fabric making two HST units (Figure C). ●

Figure C

EIGHT-AT-A-TIME HALF-SQUARE TRIANGLES

Half-square triangles (HSTs) are a basic unit of quilting used in many blocks or on their own. This construction method will yield eight HST units.

1. Refer to the pattern for size to cut squares. The standard formula is to add 1" to the finished size of the square then multiply by 2. Cut two squares from different colors this size. For example, for a 3" finished HST unit, cut 8" squares (3" + 1" = 4"; 4" x 2 = 8").

2. Draw two diagonal lines from corner to corner on the wrong side of the lightest color square. Layer the squares

right sides together. Stitch ¼" on either side of both drawn lines (Figure A).

Figure A

3. Cut the sewn squares in half horizontally and vertically, making four squares. Then cut each square apart on the drawn line, leaving a ¼" seam allowance and making eight HST units referring to Figure B. Trim each HST unit to the desired size (3½" in this example).

Figure B

4. Open the HST units and press seam allowances toward the darker fabric making eight HST units (Figure C). ●

Figure C

SEW & FLIP FLYING GEESE

With this method, squares are sewn onto opposite ends of a rectangle. The rectangle will be the center of the flying geese unit and the squares will become the "wings." After sewing in place, the squares are trimmed and flipped open to create the unit. The bias edges aren't exposed until after sewing so there is no concern about stretch and distortion.

Cutting
Refer to the pattern for the sizes to cut the rectangle and squares. Cut as directed in the pattern.

Determine the finished size of the flying geese unit you'd like to make and add ½" to the desired finished height and width of the flying geese unit, then cut a rectangle that size.

Cut two squares the same size as the height of the cut rectangle.

For example, to make one 2" x 4" finished flying geese unit, cut a 2½" x 4½" rectangle and two 2½" squares (Photo A).

Photo A

Assembly
1. Draw a diagonal line from corner to corner on the wrong side of each small square.

Place a square, right sides together, on one end of the rectangle. Sew just outside the drawn line (Photo B).

Photo B

2. Using a rotary cutter, trim ¼" away from sewn line.

Open and press to reveal the corner triangle or wing (Photo C).

Photo C

3. Place the second square, right sides together, on the opposite end of the rectangle. This square will slightly overlap the previous piece.

Sew just outside the drawn line and trim ¼" away from sewn line as before.

Open and press to complete the flying geese unit (Photo D).

Photo D

4. If desired, square up the finished unit to the required unfinished size. ●

SEW & FLIP CORNERS

Use this method to add triangle corners in a quilt block.

1. Draw a diagonal line from corner to corner on the wrong side of the specified square. Place the square, right sides together, on the indicated corner of the larger piece, making sure the line is oriented in the correct direction indicated by the pattern (Figure 1).

2. Sew on the drawn line. Trim ¼" away from sewn line (Figure 2).

3. Open and press to reveal the corner triangle (Figure 3).

Figure 1

Figure 2

Figure 3

4. If desired, square up the finished unit to the required unfinished size. ●

Supplies

We would like to thank the following manufacturers who provided materials to our designers to make sample projects for this book.

Homemade Cinnamon Rolls, page 2
Fabric from the Daisy Lane by Kansas Troubles Quilters and Jelly & Jam by Fig Tree Quilts collections for Moda Fabrics; Tuscany Silk batting from Hobbs; Aurifil 50 wt. thread.

Apple Petit Fours, page 7
Fabric from the Rainbow Spice collection by Sariditty for Moda Fabrics; Aurifil 50 wt. thread; Tuscany Silk batting from Hobbs.

Blueberry Orange Bread, page 12
Fabric from the Denim & Daisies and Jelly & Jam collections by Fig Tree Quilts for Moda Fabrics; Aurifil 50 wt. thread; Tuscany Silk batting from Hobbs.

Apple Turnover, page 16
Fabric from the Lydia's Lace collection by Betsy Chutchian for Moda Fabrics; Tuscany Silk batting from Hobbs; Aurifil 50 wt. thread.

Chocolate Cream Pie, page 21
Fabric from the Jelly & Jam and Denim & Daisies collections by Fig Tree Quilts for Moda Fabrics and Bella Solids by Moda Fabrics; Aurifil 50 wt. thread; Tuscany Silk batting from Hobbs.

Pumpkin Pancakes, page 27
Fabric from the Denim & Daisies collection by Fig Tree Quilts for Moda Fabrics; Aurifil 50 wt. thread; Tuscany Silk batting from Hobbs.

Italian Cream Cake, page 33
Fabric from the Favorite Things collection by Cheri & Chelsi for Moda Fabrics; Aurifil 50 wt. thread; Tuscany Silk batting from Hobbs.

Pecan Pie, page 37
Fabric from the Folk & Lore collection by Fancy That Design House for Moda Fabrics; Aurifil 50 wt. thread; Tuscany Silk batting from Hobbs.

Pumpkin Pie, page 41
Fabric from Bella Solids by Moda Fabrics; Aurifil 50 wt. thread; Tuscany Silk batting from Hobbs.

Annie's® Published by Annie's, 306 East Parr Road, Berne, IN 46711. Printed in USA. Copyright © 2024 Annie's. All rights reserved. This publication may not be reproduced in part or in whole without written permission from the publisher.

RETAIL STORES: If you would like to carry this publication or any other Annie's publications, visit AnniesWSL.com.

Every effort has been made to ensure that the instructions in this publication are complete and accurate. We cannot, however, take responsibility for human error, typographical mistakes or variations in individual work. Please visit AnniesCustomerService.com to check for pattern updates.

ISBN: 979-8-89253-357-7

1 2 3 4 5 6 7 8 9